# CHRISTMAS TIME IS HERE

## 7 Arrangements for Brass Quintet

### Selections from The Canadian Brass CD
### (Opening Day Entertainment Group)

ISBN 978-1-4803-6026-6

### THE CANADIAN

DISTRIBUTED BY

7777 W. BLUEMOUND RD. P.O. BOX 13819 MILWAUKEE, WI 53213

www.canadianbrass.com
www.halleonard.com

# CONTENTS

# ANGEL CHOIR AND THE TRUMPETER

Music and Lyrics by Chris Dedrick
Adapted by Chris Coletti

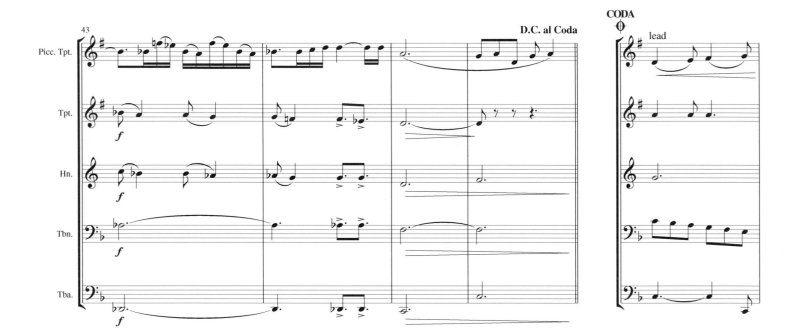

# BACH'S BELLS

Inspired by Bach's BWV 29 and
Leontovych's CAROL OF THE BELLS

Chris Coletti

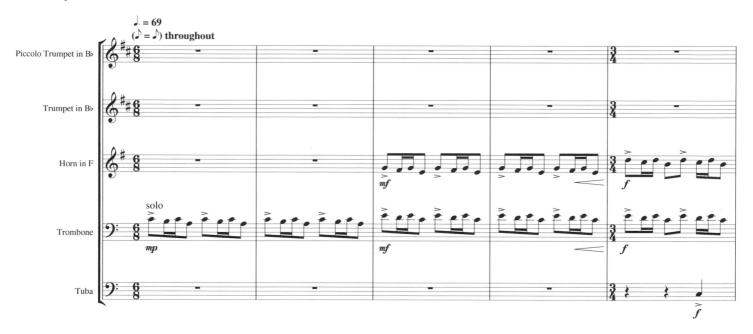

# HARK, THE HERALD ANGELS SING

Felix Mendelssohn
Arranged by Brandon Ridenour

# MY LITTLE DRUM

By Vince Guaraldi
Arranged and adapted by Brandon Ridenour

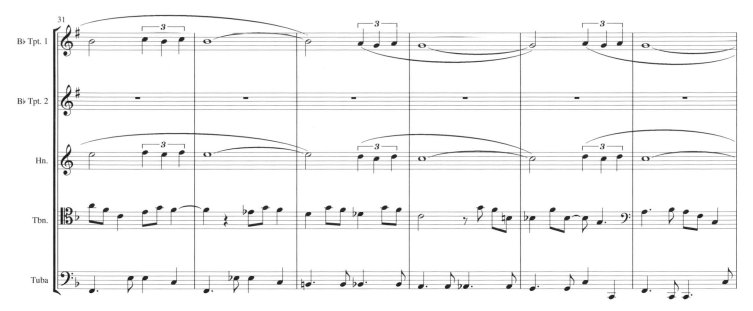

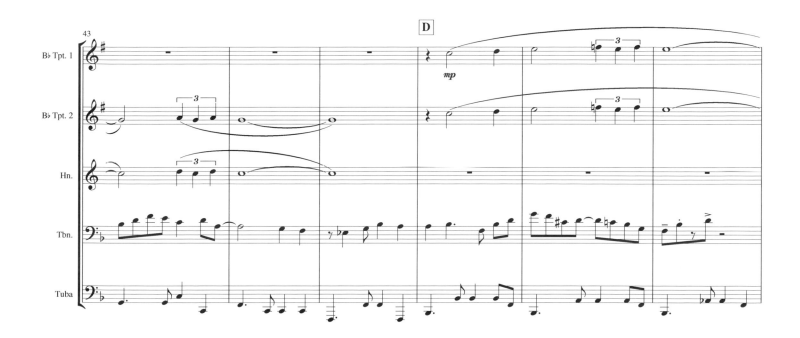

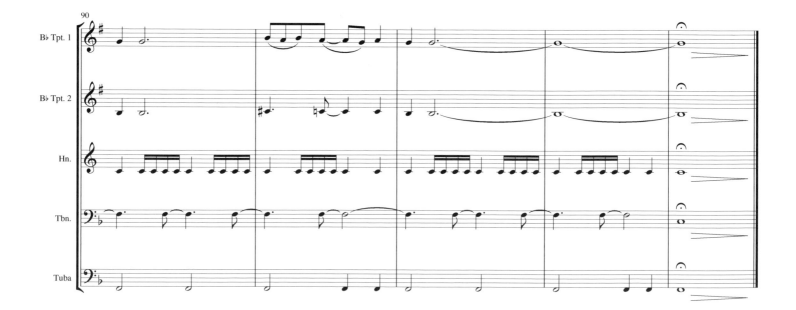

# O TANNENBAUM

Traditional
Arranged by Vince Guaraldi
Adapted by Brandon Ridenour

# SKATING

By Vince Guaraldi
Arranged by Brandon Ridenour

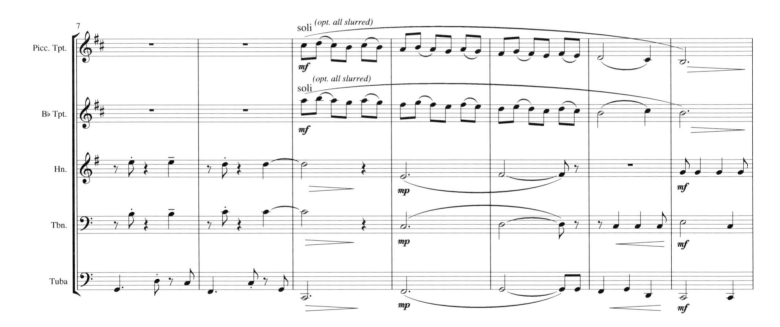

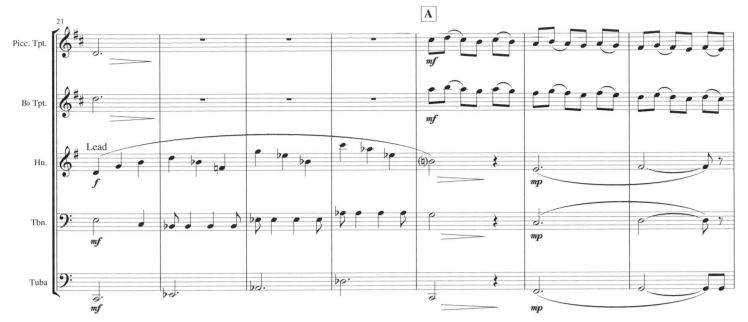

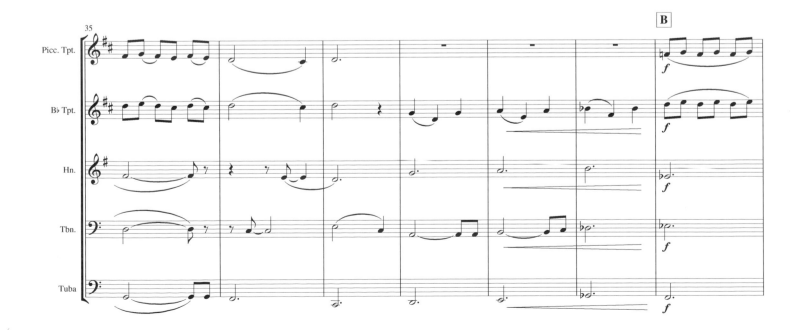

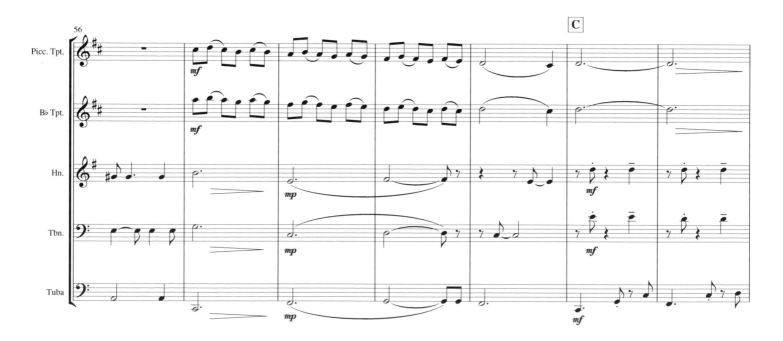

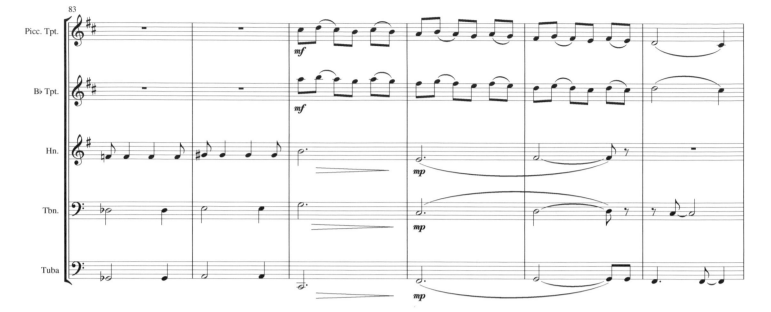

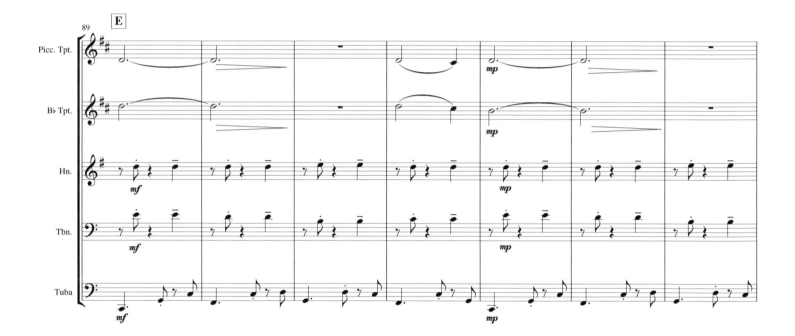

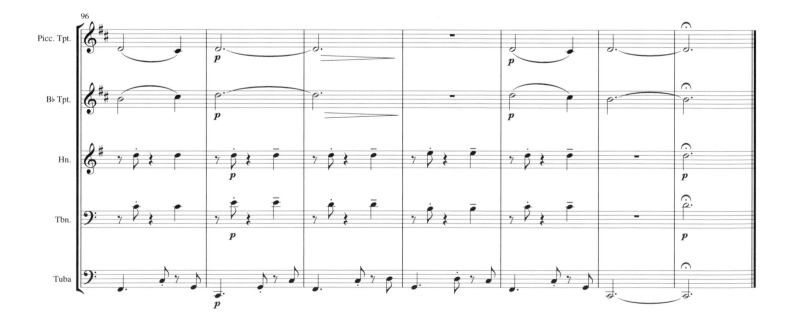

# WHAT CHILD IS THIS?

Traditional
Arranged and adapted by Brandon Ridenour

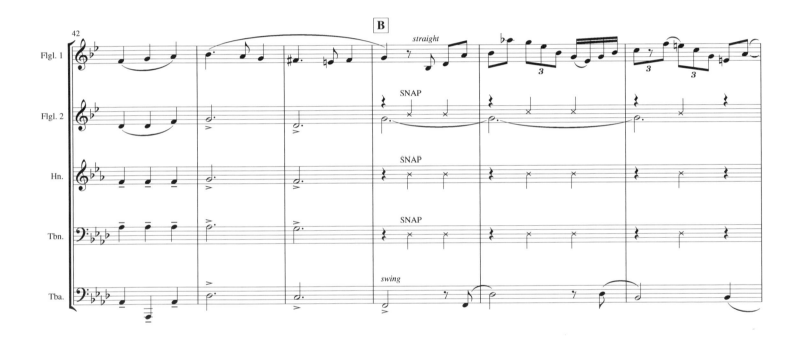

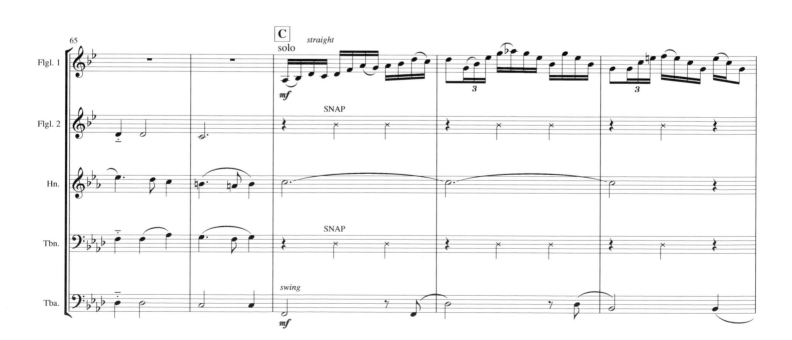

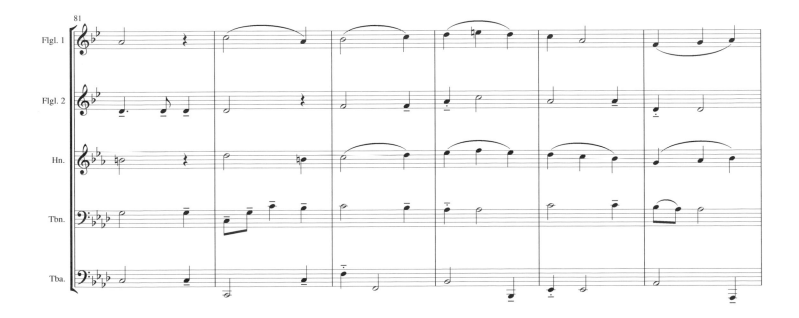

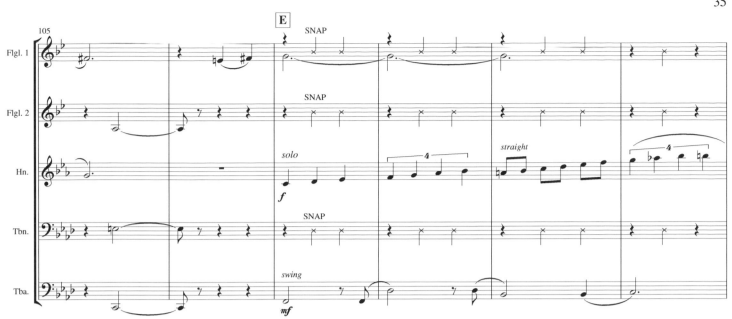

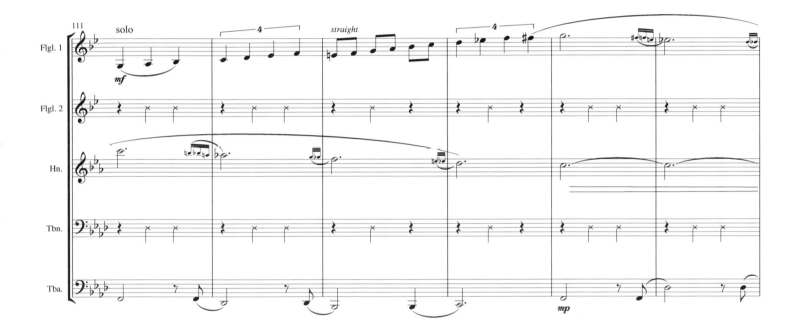

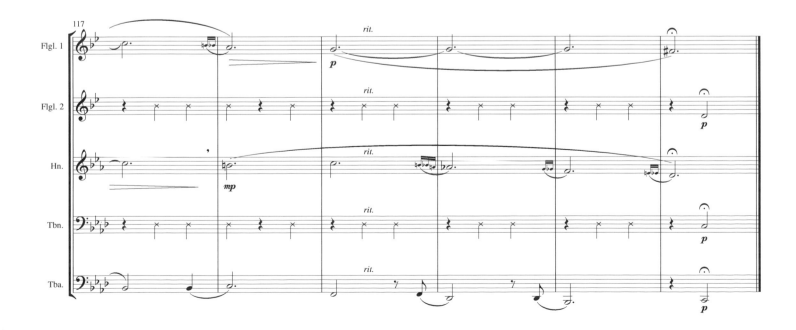